Information Technology

Introduction to Information Technology and Beyond AI

How Can You Master Information Technology Modern Best Practices?

MARK JOHN LADO

ISBN: 9798316689804

www.markjohnlado.com

DEDICATION

This book is dedicated to all the passionate learners, educators, and innovators who continue to shape the future of technology. To the students striving to understand the complexities of IT and AI, may this book serve as a guiding light in your journey. To the educators and mentors who inspire curiosity and critical thinking, your dedication fuels the next generation of tech pioneers.

A special dedication goes to my family and friends, whose unwavering support and encouragement have been my foundation. Your belief in my vision has kept me motivated throughout this journey.

Lastly, to the pioneers of information technology and artificial intelligence—those whose groundbreaking work laid the foundation for our digital world—this book stands as a tribute to your brilliance. May we continue to push the boundaries of innovation for the betterment of society.

ACKNOWLEDGMENTS

This book would not have been possible without the invaluable contributions and support of many individuals.

I extend my deepest gratitude to my mentors, colleagues, and fellow researchers whose insights and expertise have helped shape the content of this book. Your feedback and discussions have been instrumental in refining the ideas presented here.

A heartfelt thank you to my family and friends for their patience, encouragement, and unwavering belief in my work. Your support has been my strength.

I also appreciate the contributions of the technology community, authors, and researchers whose work has provided the foundation for this book. Their dedication to advancing knowledge in IT and AI has been a constant source of inspiration.

Finally, to my readers—whether you are students, professionals, or tech enthusiasts—I hope this book enriches your understanding and ignites your passion for technology. Thank you for being part of this journey.

Table of Contents

Chapter 1: Foundations of Information Technology

1.1 Definition and Importance of IT

Information Technology (IT) is broadly defined as the application of computers and telecommunications equipment to store, retrieve, transmit, and manipulate data, often in the context of a business or other[1] enterprise. It encompasses a wide range of technologies, including hardware, software, networks, and the internet, all working together to manage and process information. While often used interchangeably with terms like "computer technology," IT has a broader scope, focusing on the practical application of these technologies to solve real-world problems and achieve specific goals. The Information Technology Association of America (ITAA) provides a more comprehensive definition: "Information Technology (IT) as defined by the Information Technology Association of America (ITAA), is 'the study, design, development, implementation, support or management of computer-based information systems, particularly[2] software applications and computer[3] hardware.'" (ITAA, n.d.). This definition highlights the multifaceted nature of IT, extending beyond mere usage to include the entire lifecycle of information systems.

The importance of IT in the modern world cannot be overstated. It serves as the backbone for countless operations across various sectors. In business, IT enables efficient communication, data analysis, automation of tasks, and the development of new products and services.

For instance, consider the rise of e-commerce platforms like Amazon (www.amazon.com). Their entire business model relies heavily on sophisticated IT infrastructure to manage inventory, process orders, handle payments, and deliver products globally. Without robust IT systems, such large-scale operations would be impossible. In healthcare, IT plays a crucial role in managing patient records, facilitating telemedicine, and supporting medical research. Electronic Health Records (EHRs), for example, streamline access to patient information, improving the efficiency and accuracy of healthcare delivery (HealthIT.gov, n.d.). Even in our daily lives, we are constantly interacting with IT, from using smartphones to access information and connect with others to relying on GPS systems for navigation. The pervasive nature of IT underscores its fundamental importance in driving innovation, improving productivity, and enhancing the quality of life. A potential question readers might have is the distinction between IT and Computer Science. While related, Computer Science is more focused on the theoretical foundations of computation and algorithms, whereas IT is concerned with the practical application of these principles to real-world systems and problems.

1.2 History of IT: From Abacus to Cloud Computing

The history of Information Technology is a fascinating journey from simple calculation tools to complex global networks. One of the earliest forms of "computing" was the abacus, dating back thousands of years. This simple device allowed for basic arithmetic operations and represents a fundamental step in the human desire to automate calculation. Over centuries, mechanical calculators like Pascal's calculator and Leibniz's stepped reckoner emerged, paving the way for more sophisticated machines. The 19th century witnessed significant advancements, including Charles Babbage's conceptualization of the Analytical Engine, often considered the first general-purpose computer, and Ada Lovelace's work, which included the first algorithm intended to be processed by a machine (Fuegi & Hafner, 2003). While these machines were largely theoretical or mechanical, they laid the groundwork for the electronic era.

The 20th century marked a revolutionary period in IT history. The invention of the transistor in the mid-20th century led to smaller, faster, and more reliable computers. This era saw the development of mainframe computers, followed by personal computers (PCs) in the 1970s and 1980s, which brought computing power to individuals and small businesses. The advent of the internet in the late 20th century transformed communication and information sharing, creating a global network that continues to evolve rapidly. The early 21st century has been characterized by the rise of mobile computing, with smartphones and tablets becoming ubiquitous, and the emergence of cloud computing. Cloud computing, where computing resources and data storage are accessed over the internet, has revolutionized how businesses and individuals interact with technology, offering scalability, flexibility, and cost-effectiveness. For example, services like Google Drive (drive.google.com) allow users to store and access their files from anywhere with an internet connection.

A step-by-step guide to using Google Drive for beginners might involve:

1. Creating a Google account (if you don't already have one).
2. Navigating to drive.google.com in your web browser.
3. Clicking the "New" button to upload files or create new documents, spreadsheets, or presentations.
4. Organizing files into folders for better management.
5. Sharing files and folders with others by clicking the share icon.

Readers might wonder about the significance of each historical stage. Each development built upon the previous ones, with innovations in hardware and software continuously driving progress and expanding the capabilities of IT.

1.3 IT in Modern Society: Impact on Business, Education, and Daily Life

The impact of IT on modern society is profound and multifaceted, touching nearly every aspect of our lives. In the realm of business, IT has become an indispensable tool for enhancing efficiency, reaching new markets, and fostering innovation. Enterprise Resource Planning (ERP) systems, for instance, integrate various business processes, such as finance, human resources, and supply chain management, into a single system, leading to improved coordination and decision-making. Companies also leverage data analytics tools to gain insights into customer behavior and market trends, enabling them to make more informed strategic decisions. The rise of remote work, facilitated by IT infrastructure and communication tools like Zoom (zoom.us), has also transformed the way businesses operate.

A simple guide to joining a Zoom meeting involves:

1. Clicking on the meeting link provided by the host.
2. If prompted, downloading and installing the Zoom application.
3. Entering the meeting ID and passcode (if required).
4. Configuring your audio and video settings.
5. Clicking "Join Meeting" to enter the session.

In education, IT has opened up new possibilities for learning and teaching. Online learning platforms, such as Coursera (www.coursera.org) and edX (www.edx.org), provide access to a vast array of courses from universities worldwide, democratizing education and making it more accessible. Interactive whiteboards, educational software, and digital resources have also enhanced the classroom experience, making learning more engaging and personalized. For example, a student learning about a historical event can access primary source documents, watch video lectures, and participate in online discussions, all thanks to IT. In our daily lives, IT has become seamlessly integrated into our routines. We rely on smartphones for communication, information access, navigation, entertainment, and even managing our finances. Social media platforms connect us with friends and family across the globe, while online banking and shopping have become commonplace. Smart home devices automate tasks and enhance convenience. However, this pervasive integration also raises important questions about privacy, security, and the potential for digital divide. Readers might ask about the ethical implications of IT. Issues such as data privacy, cybersecurity threats, and the potential for job displacement due to automation are significant concerns that need[4] careful consideration and responsible development and deployment of IT.

1.4 Basic IT Terminology and Concepts

Understanding basic IT terminology and concepts is crucial for anyone studying or working in the field. Here are a few fundamental terms:

- **Hardware:** The physical components of a computer system, such as the central processing unit (CPU), memory (RAM), hard drive, monitor, keyboard, and mouse.[5]
- **Software:** The set of instructions or programs that tell the hardware what to do. Software can be broadly categorized into system software (e.g., operating systems like Windows or macOS) and application software (e.g., word processors, web browsers).
- **Network:** A system of interconnected computers and devices that can communicate and share resources. The internet is the largest example of a global network.
- **Internet:** A global network of computer networks that uses the Internet Protocol suite (TCP/IP) to communicate between devices.
- **World Wide Web (WWW):** An information system on the internet that allows documents and other resources to be interconnected by hypertext links, enabling users to easily navigate between them using a web browser.

- **Database:** An organized collection of structured information, or data, typically stored electronically in a computer system.[6] Databases are essential for managing and retrieving large amounts of data efficiently.
- **Algorithm:** A step-by-step procedure or set of rules to solve a problem or accomplish a specific task. Algorithms are the foundation of computer programming.
- **Programming Language:** A formal language comprising a set of instructions that produce various kinds of output. Programming languages are used to create software[7] applications. Examples include Python, Java, and C++.
- **Operating System (OS):** System software that manages computer hardware and software resources and provides common services for computer programs.[8] Examples include Windows, macOS, and Linux.[9]
- **Cloud Computing:** The delivery of computing services—including servers, storage, databases, networking, software, analytics, and intelligence—over the Internet ("the cloud").[10]

These are just a few of the foundational terms in IT. Understanding these concepts provides a solid base for further exploration of more advanced topics. Readers might wonder how these concepts are interconnected. For example, software runs on hardware, and networks allow hardware and software to communicate and share data. The internet is a specific type of network that enables access to the World Wide Web, which is a collection of information accessed through web browser software. Databases store the data that applications use, and algorithms written in programming languages define how software operates. A comprehensive glossary of IT terms can be found at resources like Techopedia (www.techopedia.com).

Chapter 2: Hardware and Software Essentials

2.1 Components of a Computer: CPU, Memory, Storage, and I/O Devices

At the heart of every computer lies a set of fundamental hardware components that work in concert to execute instructions and process data. Understanding these components is crucial for anyone studying Information Technology. The core elements include the Central Processing Unit (CPU), Memory (RAM), Storage, and Input/Output (I/O) devices. Think of the CPU as the "brain" of the computer. It is responsible for executing instructions from software, performing calculations, and controlling the operations of all other components. Its performance, often measured in clock speed (GHz) and the number of cores, directly impacts how quickly a computer can perform tasks. For example, when you open an application or browse a webpage, the CPU is actively processing the code and data associated with that action. A real-world scenario would be video editing; a more powerful CPU will significantly reduce the time it takes to render complex video projects.

Memory, specifically Random Access Memory (RAM), serves as the computer's short-term workspace. When you open an application or a file, it is loaded into RAM so that the CPU can access it quickly. Unlike storage, which retains data even when the power is off, RAM is volatile, meaning its contents are erased when the computer is turned off. The amount of RAM available determines how many applications can be run simultaneously and how efficiently the computer can multitask. Imagine RAM as your desk space; a larger desk allows you to have more documents and tools readily available for immediate use. A common challenge users face is a slow computer due to insufficient RAM. Upgrading the RAM is often a cost-effective solution to improve performance in such cases. Storage devices, such as Hard Disk Drives (HDDs) or Solid State Drives (SSDs), are used for long-term data storage. This is where your operating system, applications, and personal files are stored permanently. SSDs are generally faster than HDDs, leading to quicker boot times and application loading. Consider the difference when starting a computer with an HDD versus an SSD; the latter often boots up in a fraction of the time. Input/Output (I/O) devices facilitate interaction between the user and the computer. Input devices allow you to provide data and instructions, such as keyboards, mice, touchscreens, and microphones. Output devices display or present the results of processing, such as monitors, printers, and speakers. For instance, when you type on a keyboard (input), the characters appear on the monitor (output). According to Tanenbaum and Austin (2013), "A typical personal computer consists of a CPU, memory, and some input/output devices connected by a bus." (p. 5). Understanding the interplay between these components is fundamental to comprehending how a computer system functions.

2.2 Operating Systems: Windows, Linux, macOS, and Mobile OS

The operating system (OS) is a crucial piece of system software that manages computer hardware and software resources and provides common services for computer[1] programs. It acts as an intermediary between the[2] user and the hardware, making it possible for applications to run. Popular desktop operating systems include Windows, Linux, and macOS, while mobile devices primarily use Android and iOS. Each OS has its own strengths, weaknesses, and target user base. Windows, developed by Microsoft, is the most widely used desktop OS globally, known for its broad software compatibility and extensive hardware support. It is commonly used in businesses, homes, and educational institutions. For example, many universities rely on Windows-based systems for their computer labs due to the availability of a wide range of academic software.

Linux, on the other hand, is an open-source OS known for its flexibility, customizability, and security. It comes in various distributions, such as Ubuntu, Fedora, and Debian, each tailored for different needs. Linux is particularly popular among developers, system administrators, and in server environments. Many web servers and cloud infrastructure rely on Linux due to its stability and command-line interface capabilities.

A practical example is setting up a web server using Ubuntu. A simplified step-by-step guide might involve:

1. Downloading the Ubuntu Server ISO image from the official website (ubuntu.com/download/server).
2. Creating a bootable USB drive using a tool like Rufus (rufus.ie/en/).
3. Booting the server from the USB drive and following the installation prompts.
4. Once installed, accessing the server via SSH (Secure Shell) using a terminal application.

5. Installing a web server software like Apache or Nginx using the command line. macOS, developed by Apple, is known for its user-friendly interface, strong integration with Apple hardware, and focus on design and creativity.

It is primarily used on Apple's line of Macintosh computers and is popular among creative professionals. Mobile operating systems like Android (developed by Google) and iOS (developed by Apple) are designed specifically for mobile devices such as smartphones and tablets. Android is the most widely used mobile OS globally, known for its open nature and wide range of device manufacturers. iOS is known for its seamless integration with Apple's hardware and its focus on user experience and security. Silberschatz, Galvin, and Gagne (2018) define an operating system as "a program that manages the computer hardware." (p. 3). Choosing the right operating system depends on individual needs, software requirements, and hardware compatibility. Readers might ask about dual-booting or virtualization as solutions for needing multiple operating systems. Dual-booting allows you to install multiple OSs on a single computer and choose which one to boot into. Virtualization software, such as VMware Workstation Player (www.vmware.com/products/workstation-player/player-evaluation.html) or VirtualBox (www.virtualbox.org), allows you to run one operating system within another, providing flexibility for testing and compatibility purposes.

A basic step-by-step guide to creating a virtual machine using VirtualBox involves:

1. Downloading and installing VirtualBox from the official website (virtualbox.org/wiki/Downloads).
2. Clicking "New" to create a new virtual machine.
3. Specifying a name for the VM, selecting the operating system type and version.
4. Allocating memory and creating a virtual hard disk.
5. Selecting the downloaded ISO image of the desired OS as the boot disk.
6. Starting the virtual machine and following the OS installation prompts.

2.3 Software Types: System Software, Application Software, and Development Tools

Software is the set of instructions that tells the computer hardware what to do. It can be broadly categorized into system software, application software, and development tools. System software manages and controls the computer's hardware and provides a platform for application software to run. The operating system itself is the most important piece of system software. Other examples include utility programs, such as file managers, disk defragmenters, and antivirus software. These utilities help manage, maintain, and protect the computer system. For instance, Windows Defender is a built-in utility in Windows that provides basic protection against malware.

Application software, on the other hand, is designed for specific tasks that users want to perform. This category includes a vast array of programs, such as word processors (e.g., Microsoft Word, Google Docs), web browsers (e.g., Google Chrome, Mozilla Firefox), spreadsheets (e.g., Microsoft Excel, Google Sheets), presentation software (e.g., Microsoft PowerPoint, Google Slides), graphics editors (e.g., Adobe Photoshop, GIMP), and games. Consider a student writing a research paper; they would use a word processor (application software) running on an operating system (system software). Development tools are used by programmers to create, test, and maintain software applications. These tools include compilers, interpreters, debuggers, integrated development environments (IDEs), and software development kits (SDKs). For example, Python is a popular programming language, and developers often use IDEs like PyCharm (www.jetbrains.com/pycharm/) to write, debug, and run Python code.

A basic step-by-step guide to running a simple Python script in PyCharm involves:

1. Downloading and installing PyCharm Community Edition from the JetBrains website.
2. Creating a new project in PyCharm.
3. Creating a new Python file within the project (e.g., hello.py).
4. Writing Python code in the file, such as print("Hello, World!").
5. Right-clicking on the file in the project explorer and selecting "Run 'hello'".

The output ("Hello, World!") will be displayed in the PyCharm console. Sommerville (2011) states that "Software engineering is concerned with all aspects of software production from the early stages of system specification through to maintaining the system after it has gone into[3] operational use." (p. 3). Development tools are essential for this entire process. Readers might ask about the relationship between these software types. System software provides the foundation for application software to run, while development tools enable the creation of both system and application software.

2.4 Emerging Trends in Hardware: Quantum Computing and Edge Computing

The field of computer hardware is constantly evolving, with new technologies emerging that promise to revolutionize computing as we know it. Two prominent emerging trends are quantum computing and edge computing. Quantum computing leverages the principles of quantum mechanics, such as superposition and entanglement, to perform calculations that are impossible for classical computers. Traditional computers store information as bits, which can be either 0 or 1. Quantum computers, on the other hand, use qubits, which can exist in a superposition of both 0 and 1 simultaneously. This allows quantum computers to explore a vast number of possibilities concurrently, making them potentially well-suited for solving complex problems in fields like drug discovery, materials science, and cryptography. While still in its early stages of development, companies like IBM (ibm.com/quantum-computing/) and Google are actively investing in quantum computing research and development. A real-world application could be the development of new catalysts for chemical reactions, which currently involves computationally intensive simulations that classical computers struggle with.

Edge computing is another significant trend that addresses the increasing need for faster data processing and reduced latency. Traditional cloud computing involves sending data from devices to centralized data centers for processing. Edge computing, in contrast, brings computation and data storage closer to the source of data generation, such as sensors, IoT devices, and user devices. This is particularly beneficial for applications that require real-time processing, such as autonomous vehicles, industrial automation, and augmented reality. For example, in a self-driving car, processing data from sensors locally in real-time is crucial for making immediate decisions and ensuring safety. Edge computing reduces the reliance on network connectivity and the latency associated with sending data to the cloud. According to Shi, Pallickara, and Jiang (2013), "Edge computing is a paradigm that extends cloud computing by performing computation at the edge of the network, closer to the data source." (p. 37). Readers might wonder about the challenges associated with these emerging technologies. Quantum computing faces challenges in terms of stability (qubit coherence) and error correction, while edge computing requires managing a large number of distributed devices and ensuring security at the edge. Despite these challenges, both quantum computing and edge computing hold immense potential to transform various industries and drive future technological advancements.

Chapter 3: The Internet, Networking, and Cybersecurity

3.1 The Internet and How It Works: TCP/IP, DNS, and HTTP

The internet, a vast global network connecting billions of devices, operates on a suite of protocols that enable seamless communication. Understanding these foundational protocols is essential for IT professionals. At the core of internet communication lies the Transmission Control Protocol/Internet Protocol (TCP/IP) suite. TCP handles the reliable transmission of data by breaking it down into smaller packets, ensuring they arrive in the correct order and retransmitting any lost packets. IP is responsible for addressing and routing these packets across the network, much like a postal system uses addresses to deliver mail. When you request a webpage, for instance, your computer sends TCP/IP packets containing your request to the web server. The server then responds with TCP/IP packets containing the webpage data. Comer (2018) aptly describes TCP/IP as "the language of the Internet" (p. 1).

Another crucial component is the Domain Name System (DNS). Humans interact with websites using domain names (e.g., google.com), which are easy to remember. However, computers communicate using IP addresses (e.g., 172.217.160.142), which are numerical. DNS acts as a phonebook for the internet, translating human-readable domain names into their corresponding IP addresses. When you type a website address into your browser, your computer first contacts a DNS server to look up the IP address associated with that domain name. Once the IP address is obtained, your computer can then connect to the web server. A practical way to observe DNS in action is using the nslookup command in a command prompt or terminal.

A step-by-step guide would be:

1. Open the command prompt (Windows) or terminal (macOS/Linux).
2. Type nslookup google.com and press Enter.
3. The output will show the IP address associated with the domain "google.com" and the DNS server that provided the information.

Finally, the Hypertext Transfer Protocol (HTTP) is the foundation of data communication on the World Wide Web. It defines how messages are formatted and transmitted[1] between web browsers and web servers. When you visit a website, your browser sends an HTTP request to the server, asking for specific content (e.g., a webpage, an image). The server then responds with an HTTP response containing the requested data. For secure communication, HTTPS (HTTP Secure) is used, which encrypts the communication between the browser and the server using protocols like TLS/SSL. This is particularly important when transmitting sensitive information like passwords or credit card details. A common question might be about network latency. Latency refers to the delay in data transfer over a network. It can be affected by various factors, including the distance between the client and server, the number of network hops, and network congestion. Tools like ping and traceroute can be used to diagnose network latency issues. For example, typing ping google.com in the command prompt will send packets to Google's server and measure the round-trip time, giving an indication of the latency.

3.2 Wireless and Wired Networks: LAN, WAN, and Cloud Networking

Computer networks facilitate the sharing of resources and information. They can be broadly classified into Local Area Networks (LANs), Wide Area Networks (WANs), and the increasingly prevalent Cloud Networking. A LAN connects devices within a limited geographical area, such as an office, a home, or a school. Common technologies used in LANs include Ethernet for wired connections and Wi-Fi (IEEE 802.11 standards) for wireless connections. In a typical office setting, computers, printers, and servers are often connected via a LAN, allowing employees to share files and access network resources.

A WAN, on the other hand, spans a much larger geographical area, connecting multiple LANs. The internet itself is the largest example of a WAN. Businesses with multiple offices in different cities or countries rely on WANs to connect their networks and enable communication and data sharing across vast distances. Technologies used in WANs include leased lines, fiber optic cables, and satellite links. For instance, a multinational corporation might use a WAN to connect its headquarters in one country with its branch offices in another.

Cloud networking refers to the network infrastructure and services that reside in the cloud. This allows organizations to build and manage their networks using resources provided by cloud service providers like

Amazon Web Services (AWS), Microsoft Azure, and Google Cloud Platform. Cloud networking offers scalability, flexibility, and cost-effectiveness, as organizations can easily scale their network resources up or down based on their needs without investing in physical infrastructure. For example, a startup might use AWS Virtual Private Cloud (VPC) to create a private network within the AWS cloud, connecting their web servers, databases, and other resources.

A step-by-step guide to creating a basic VPC in AWS involves:

1. Logging into the AWS Management Console and navigating to the VPC service.
2. Clicking "Create VPC" and choosing the "VPC only" option.
3. Specifying a CIDR block (a range of IP addresses) for your VPC.
4. Creating subnets within the VPC in different Availability Zones for redundancy.
5. Setting up an Internet Gateway and attaching it to your VPC to allow internet access.
6. Configuring Route Tables to direct traffic within your VPC and to the internet.

Stallings and Case (2016) highlight the increasing importance of cloud networking, stating that "Cloud computing is transforming the way organizations deploy and manage their IT resources, and networking is a critical component of this transformation." (p. 457). A potential question might be about the advantages and disadvantages of wired versus wireless networks. Wired networks generally offer higher speeds, lower latency, and more stable connections, but they lack the mobility and flexibility of wireless networks. Wireless networks, while convenient, can be more susceptible to interference and security vulnerabilities if not properly configured.

3.3 Cyber Threats and Security: Malware, Phishing, and Ransomware

In the digital age, cyber threats pose significant risks to individuals, businesses, and governments. Understanding common threats and how they work is crucial for implementing effective security measures. Malware, short for malicious software, is a broad term encompassing various types of harmful software designed to disrupt, damage, or gain unauthorized access to a computer system. This includes viruses, which attach themselves to legitimate files and spread when those files are executed; worms, which can self-replicate and spread across networks without requiring a host file; and Trojans, which disguise themselves as legitimate software to trick users into installing them, often containing backdoors or other malicious functionalities. A real-world example is the WannaCry ransomware attack in 2017, which spread rapidly across networks, encrypting files and demanding a ransom in Bitcoin for their decryption.

Phishing is a type of social engineering attack where attackers attempt to deceive individuals into revealing sensitive information,[3] such as usernames, passwords, and credit card details, by impersonating legitimate entities like banks or online service providers. These attacks often come in the form of emails, text messages, or phone calls that look genuine. For instance, a common phishing email might claim that your bank account has been compromised and ask you to click on a link to verify your details, leading to a fake website designed to steal your login credentials.

Ransomware is a specific type of malware that encrypts a victim's files and demands a ransom payment, typically in cryptocurrency, in exchange for the decryption key. Ransomware attacks can be devastating for individuals and organizations, leading to significant[4] data loss and financial costs. The Colonial Pipeline attack in 2021, where ransomware disrupted a major fuel pipeline in the United States, highlights the potential real-world impact of such attacks. According to Verizon's 2023 Data Breach Investigations Report (DBIR), "Ransomware continues to be a significant threat, with an increase in both frequency and impact across various industries." (Verizon, 2023, p. 12). A potential question might be how to identify these threats. Being cautious about unsolicited emails or messages, verifying the sender's authenticity, and avoiding clicking on suspicious links or downloading attachments from unknown sources are crucial steps in preventing these attacks. Keeping software up to date with the latest security patches is also essential, as these patches often address known vulnerabilities that malware can exploit.

3.4 Cybersecurity Best Practices: Encryption, Firewalls, and Ethical Hacking

Implementing robust cybersecurity best practices is essential for protecting systems and data from the threats discussed earlier. Encryption is a fundamental security measure that converts data into an unreadable format, called ciphertext, making it incomprehensible to unauthorized individuals. This ensures that even if data is intercepted, it cannot be understood without the correct decryption key. Encryption is used in various contexts, such as securing network communication (e.g., HTTPS), protecting data stored on devices (e.g., full-disk encryption), and securing email communication (e.g., PGP/GPG). For example, when you access a website with "https://" in the address bar, your communication with the website is encrypted using TLS/SSL.

Firewalls act as a security barrier between a network and the outside world, monitoring incoming and outgoing network traffic and blocking any traffic that does not meet predefined security rules. Firewalls can be hardware-based, software-based (often integrated into operating systems), or cloud-based. They are a critical line of defense against unauthorized access to a network or individual computer. Most modern operating systems, such as Windows and macOS, include built-in software firewalls that can be configured to control network access.

Ethical hacking, also known as penetration testing, involves simulating real-world cyberattacks on a system or network to identify vulnerabilities that[5] could be exploited by malicious actors. Ethical hackers use the same tools and techniques as attackers but with the permission of the organization to improve its security posture. The findings from ethical hacking exercises help organizations understand their weaknesses and implement appropriate security controls. For example, a company might hire a team of ethical hackers to conduct a penetration test on its web application to identify and fix any security flaws before they can be exploited by cybercriminals. Whitman and Mattord (2020) define ethical hacking as "the process of attempting to gain access to resources of an organization without the consent of the owners, but with their knowledge and approval." (p. 45). A potential question might be about the limitations of these practices. While encryption, firewalls, and ethical hacking are crucial security measures, they are not foolproof. Security is an ongoing process that requires continuous monitoring, adaptation, and user awareness training to stay ahead of evolving threats. Organizations also need to implement other best practices, such as strong password policies, multi-factor authentication, and regular security audits, to create a comprehensive security posture.

Chapter 4: Data and Databases in the Digital Age

4.1 Data Types: Structured, Unstructured, and Semi-Structured Data

In the digital age, data is the lifeblood of information systems. Understanding the different types of data is fundamental to managing and leveraging it effectively. Data can be broadly categorized into three main types: structured, unstructured, and semi-structured. Structured data is highly organized and typically stored in relational databases. It adheres to a predefined schema, making it easy to search, analyze, and manage. Examples include customer records in a CRM system, financial transaction data, and inventory information in a retail database. Each piece of data fits neatly into defined fields and tables, allowing for efficient querying using languages like SQL. For instance, an online retailer might have a database table with columns for customer ID, name, address, and purchase history, all of which are well-defined and organized.

Unstructured data, on the other hand, does not have a predefined format or organization. It is often text-heavy but can also include multimedia content such as images, videos, and audio files. Examples include social media posts, emails, blog articles, and customer reviews. Analyzing unstructured data can be more challenging but often yields valuable insights into customer sentiment, emerging trends, and complex relationships. Consider the vast amounts of text data generated daily on platforms like Twitter (now X, www.x.com). Analyzing these tweets can provide real-time insights into public opinion about a particular product or event.

Semi-structured data falls between structured and unstructured data. It doesn't conform to a rigid schema like structured data but contains tags or markers that separate semantic elements and enforce hierarchies of records and fields within the data. Examples include JSON (JavaScript Object Notation),[1] XML (Extensible Markup Language), and CSV (Comma Separated Values) files. These formats[2] provide a level of organization that makes it easier to parse and analyze compared to completely unstructured data. For instance, a product catalog might be stored in a JSON format, where each product has attributes like name, description, price, and images, all tagged within the JSON structure. According to Loshin (2013), "Data can be classified based on its format and structure, which impacts how it can be stored, processed, and analyzed." (p. 27). A potential question readers might have is how to convert data from one type to another. Data transformation processes are often used to convert data between different formats, depending on the requirements of the analysis or the target system. For example, unstructured text data might be processed using Natural Language Processing (NLP) techniques to extract structured information like keywords or sentiment scores.

4.2 Database Management Systems (DBMS): SQL vs. NoSQL

A Database Management System (DBMS) is software used to manage, store, and retrieve data in a database. Two primary categories of DBMS have emerged: those based on the relational model using SQL (Structured Query Language) and those that are non-relational, often referred to as NoSQL (Not only SQL) databases. SQL databases, such as MySQL, PostgreSQL, and Oracle, are based on a structured schema with tables consisting of rows and columns. They are highly effective for managing structured data and are known for their data integrity, consistency, and support for complex queries using SQL. Relational databases are well-suited for applications with well-defined data structures and complex relationships between data, such as online transaction processing (OLTP) systems used in e-commerce or banking. For example, an online store would use a relational database to manage customer orders, product inventory, and shipping information, ensuring data consistency across all related tables.

NoSQL databases, on the other hand, are designed to handle large volumes of unstructured or semi-structured data with high scalability and performance. They come in various types, including document databases (e.g., MongoDB), key-value stores (e.g., Redis), column-family databases (e.g., Cassandra), and graph databases (e.g., Neo4j). Each type is optimized for specific use cases. For instance, MongoDB, a document database, is often used for content management systems or applications with flexible and evolving data models, where data can be stored in JSON-like documents. Redis, a key-value store, is frequently used for caching to improve application performance by storing frequently accessed data in memory. Stonebraker and Kemper (2011) argue that "No single database architecture is optimal for all workloads, leading to the rise of specialized NoSQL systems." (p. 90). A common question might be when to choose between SQL and NoSQL. The choice depends on the specific requirements of the application, including the type of data, the volume of data, the need for scalability, and the complexity of the queries. If the data is highly structured with clear relationships and requires strong consistency, an SQL database is often the better choice. If the data is unstructured or semi-structured, requires high scalability and availability, and complex relationships are less critical, a NoSQL database might be more appropriate. Exploring different database systems can be done using online platforms like MongoDB Atlas (www.mongodb.com/cloud/atlas/signup) which offers a free tier to experiment with MongoDB.

A step-by-step guide to creating a free MongoDB Atlas cluster involves:

1. Signing up for a free account on the MongoDB Atlas website.
2. Clicking the "Build a Database" button.
3. Choosing the "Shared" tier (free tier) and selecting your preferred cloud provider and region.
4. Configuring the cluster name and clicking "Create Cluster".
5. Once the cluster is created, you can connect to it using the provided connection string and start working with MongoDB documents.

4.3 Data Science and Big Data: Analyzing Large-Scale Information

Data science is an interdisciplinary field that uses scientific methods, processes, algorithms,[4] and systems to extract knowledge and insights from noisy,[5] structured, and unstructured data, and apply that knowledge across a broad range of application domains. It involves a combination of statistics, computer science, and domain expertise to analyze large and complex datasets. Big data refers to extremely large data sets that may be analyzed computationally to reveal[6] patterns, trends, and associations, especially relating to human behavior and[7] interactions. These datasets are characterized by the "Five Vs": Volume (massive amounts of data), Velocity (data generated at a high speed), Variety (different types of data), Veracity (data quality and accuracy), and Value (the potential insights and business benefits).

The applications of data science and big data are vast and span across various industries. In e-commerce, data science is used for personalized recommendations, fraud detection, and predicting customer behavior. For example, Amazon (www.amazon.com) uses sophisticated algorithms to analyze past purchase history and Browse behavior to suggest products that customers might be interested in. In healthcare, big data analytics can help identify disease patterns, improve diagnostic accuracy, and personalize treatment plans. For instance, analyzing large datasets of patient records can help researchers identify risk factors for certain diseases. In finance, data science is used for algorithmic trading, risk management, and fraud prevention. Provost and Fawcett (2013) emphasize the importance of data science, stating that "Data science has emerged as a critical component of business intelligence and analytics, enabling organizations to make data-driven decisions." (p. 1). A potential question might be about the tools and techniques used in data science. Data scientists use a variety of tools and programming languages, including Python, R, and SQL, along with libraries and frameworks for data manipulation, statistical analysis, machine learning, and data visualization. For example, Python libraries like Pandas, NumPy, Scikit-learn, and Matplotlib are widely used in the data science community. Exploring these tools often involves hands-on practice. For instance, getting started with Pandas for data manipulation can be done by installing the library in Python using `pip install pandas` and then experimenting with reading data from CSV files, cleaning and transforming data, and performing basic analysis using Pandas DataFrames. Numerous online tutorials and resources, such as the official Pandas documentation (pandas.pydata.org/docs/user_guide/10min.html), provide step-by-step guidance for learning these tools.

4.4 Data Privacy and Ethics in the AI Era

The increasing volume and complexity of data, coupled with the rise of artificial intelligence (AI), have brought data privacy and ethics to the forefront of IT considerations. Data privacy concerns the rights of individuals to control the collection, use, and sharing of their personal information. Regulations like the General Data Protection Regulation (GDPR) in the European Union and[8] the California Consumer Privacy Act (CCPA) in the United States have been enacted to protect individuals' data privacy rights. These regulations impose strict requirements on organizations regarding data collection, consent, data security, and the right to be forgotten.

Ethics in the context of data and AI involves considering the moral principles and societal implications of how data is collected, analyzed, and used, especially in AI systems. Biases in training data can lead to unfair or discriminatory outcomes in AI applications, such as facial recognition systems or loan approval algorithms. Ensuring fairness, transparency, and accountability in AI systems is a critical ethical challenge. For example, if an AI system used for hiring is trained on historical data that reflects gender bias, it might perpetuate this bias in its recommendations. O'Neil (2016) highlights these concerns in her book "Weapons of Math Destruction," arguing that algorithms can encode and amplify societal biases. A potential question might be about how to ensure data privacy and ethical practices in AI development. Implementing techniques like anonymization and pseudonymization can help protect individual privacy. Organizations also need to establish clear ethical guidelines for data collection and use, ensure transparency in how AI systems work, and regularly audit these systems for bias and fairness. Furthermore, obtaining informed consent from individuals before collecting and using their data is a fundamental ethical principle. Resources like the AI Ethics Guidelines developed by the European Union (ec.europa.eu/newsroom/dae/redirection/document/6687) provide frameworks for addressing these complex issues. Engaging in discussions about the societal impact of AI and promoting responsible AI development practices are crucial for navigating the ethical challenges of the AI era.

Chapter 5: Artificial Intelligence: From Basics to Deep Learning

5.1 What is AI? Definitions and Key Concepts

Artificial Intelligence (AI) is a broad field encompassing the theory and development of computer systems able to perform tasks that typically require human intelligence, such as learning, problem-solving, decision-making, and understanding natural language.[1] There isn't a single universally accepted definition, but a common thread across various definitions is the ability of machines to mimic cognitive functions. Russell and Norvig (2020) offer a comprehensive perspective, defining AI through four possible goals: systems that think like humans, systems that think rationally, systems that act like humans, and systems that act rationally[2] (p. 2). Thinking like humans involves creating machines that can replicate the cognitive processes of the human mind, often explored in cognitive science. Thinking rationally focuses on creating systems that can make logical inferences and solve problems optimally, as studied in logic and philosophy. Acting like humans, exemplified by the Turing Test proposed by Alan Turing, aims to build machines whose behavior is indistinguishable from that of a human. Acting rationally, the ideal often pursued in AI research, involves designing systems that can achieve their goals given their beliefs.

Several key concepts underpin the field of AI. An **agent** is anything that can perceive its environment through sensors and act upon that environment through actuators.[3] A human agent has eyes, ears, and other sensory organs as sensors, and hands, legs, and a mouth as actuators. A robotic agent might have cameras and infrared range finders as sensors and various motors and effectors as actuators. The **environment** is the surroundings in which the agent operates. Environments can be fully observable or partially observable, deterministic or stochastic, episodic or sequential, static or dynamic, discrete or continuous, and single-agent[4] or multi-agent. **Rationality** in AI refers to the ability of an agent to choose actions that are expected to maximize its performance measure, given its percept sequence (history of what it has perceived), its knowledge, and the actions it can perform. The **Turing Test**, proposed by Alan Turing in 1950, provides an operational definition of intelligence: a machine exhibits intelligent behavior if a human evaluator cannot reliably distinguish between the machine's responses and those of a human respondent when both are asked the same questions. While the Turing Test remains a significant philosophical benchmark, modern AI research often focuses on more specific and measurable tasks. A potential question readers might have is about the difference between "strong AI" (or Artificial General Intelligence - AGI) and "weak AI" (or Narrow AI). Weak AI focuses on performing specific tasks intelligently, such as playing chess or recognizing faces, and this is where most current AI applications reside. Strong AI, on the other hand, aims to create machines with human-level general intelligence, capable of performing any intellectual task that a human being can. This remains a significant long-term goal of AI research.

5.2 Machine Learning vs. Deep Learning

Machine Learning (ML) is a subfield of AI that focuses on enabling computers to learn from data without being explicitly programmed. Instead of writing specific rules for every possible scenario, ML algorithms learn patterns and relationships in data to make predictions or decisions. A classic example of machine learning is spam filtering. By analyzing a large dataset of emails labeled as "spam" or "not spam," an ML algorithm can learn to identify characteristics of spam emails and automatically filter them out. Bishop (2006) defines machine learning as "a field that is concerned with the question of how to construct computer programs that automatically improve through experience" (p. 1). Common machine learning algorithms include linear regression, logistic regression, support vector machines, decision trees,[5] and random forests.

Deep Learning (DL) is a subfield of machine learning that utilizes artificial neural networks with multiple layers (hence, "deep") to learn complex patterns from large amounts of data. These neural networks are inspired by the structure and function of the human brain. Deep learning has achieved remarkable success in tasks such as[6] image recognition, natural language processing, and speech recognition, where traditional machine learning algorithms[7] often struggled. For instance, in image recognition, a deep learning model can be trained on millions of images to accurately identify objects, animals, and people. LeCun, Bengio, and Hinton (2015) highlight the impact of deep learning, stating that "Deep learning allows computational models that are composed of multiple processing layers to learn representations of data with multiple levels of abstraction."[8] (p. 436). The key difference between traditional machine learning and deep learning lies in how features are extracted from the data. In traditional ML, domain experts often need to manually engineer relevant features for the algorithm to learn from. In deep learning, these features are automatically learned by the deep neural network from raw data. For example, in image recognition using traditional ML, features like edges, corners, and textures might need to be extracted manually before being fed into a classifier. In deep learning, the convolutional layers of a deep neural network automatically learn these hierarchical features from the pixel data. A potential question readers might have is when to use machine learning versus deep learning. Deep learning typically requires large amounts of data and significant computational resources (like GPUs) to train effectively, but it can achieve state-of-the-art results in complex tasks. Traditional machine learning algorithms can often perform well with smaller datasets and are more interpretable, making them suitable for applications where understanding the reasoning behind a prediction is important. Getting started with deep learning can be done using frameworks like TensorFlow (www.tensorflow.org) or PyTorch (pytorch.org).

For example, a basic step-by-step guide to training a simple neural network for image classification using TensorFlow and Keras might involve:

1. Installing TensorFlow using pip install tensorflow.
2. Loading a dataset like MNIST (handwritten digits) using tf.keras.datasets.mnist.load_data().
3. Preprocessing the data by normalizing pixel values.

4. Defining a neural network model using tf.keras.models.Sequential with layers like tf.keras.layers.Dense.
5. Compiling the model by specifying an optimizer, loss function, and metrics.
6. Training the model using model.fit() with the training data and labels.
7. Evaluating the model's performance using model.evaluate() with the test data and labels.

5.3 Natural Language Processing (NLP) and AI in Communication

Natural Language Processing (NLP) is a field of AI that focuses on enabling computers to understand, interpret, and generate human language.[9] The goal of NLP is to bridge the gap between human communication and computer understanding.[10] This involves a wide range of tasks, including sentiment analysis (determining the emotional tone of text), machine translation (converting text from one language to another), text summarization (creating concise summaries of longer texts), and question answering (enabling computers to answer questions posed in natural language). Jurafsky and Martin (2023) provide a comprehensive overview of the field, defining NLP as "a field of computer science, artificial intelligence, and computational linguistics concerned with the interactions between computers and human (natural) languages."[11] (p. 1).

AI has significantly impacted communication through various NLP applications. Chatbots, for instance, use NLP to understand user queries and provide automated responses, often used for customer service or information retrieval on websites. Virtual assistants like Siri, Alexa, and Google Assistant utilize NLP for voice recognition, understanding commands, and providing information or performing tasks. Machine translation services like Google Translate (translate.google.com) leverage NLP to translate text and speech between numerous languages.

A step-by-step guide to using Google Translate for basic text translation involves:

1. Navigating to translate.google.com in your web browser.
2. Selecting the source language (or letting the system detect it automatically) and the target language.
3. Typing or pasting the text you want to translate into the left-hand box.
4. The translated text will appear automatically in the right-hand box.

More advanced features include voice input and output, as well as document translation. A potential question readers might have is about the challenges of NLP. Human language is inherently complex, with nuances like sarcasm, ambiguity, and context-dependent meaning that can be difficult for computers to understand. For example, the sentence "Time flies like an arrow" can be interpreted in different ways. NLP researchers are constantly working on developing more sophisticated models that can better handle these complexities. Techniques like deep learning have significantly improved the performance of NLP tasks, allowing for more accurate and context-aware language understanding and generation.

5.4 AI Applications: Healthcare, Finance, and Autonomous Vehicles

AI is rapidly transforming various industries, offering innovative solutions and improving efficiency. In **healthcare**, AI is being used for a wide range of applications, including medical image analysis (e.g., detecting tumors in X-rays or MRIs), drug discovery and development (e.g., identifying potential drug candidates and predicting their efficacy), personalized medicine (e.g., tailoring treatment plans based on individual patient data), and robotic surgery (e.g., assisting surgeons with complex procedures). For example, AI algorithms can analyze medical images with high accuracy, sometimes even surpassing human capabilities in detecting subtle anomalies. Topol (2019) discusses the transformative potential of AI in medicine, stating that "AI will change virtually every aspect of how medicine is practiced and delivered." (p. 3).

In **finance**, AI is being deployed for tasks such as fraud detection (e.g., identifying unusual transaction patterns), algorithmic trading (e.g., using AI models to make automated trading decisions), risk assessment (e.g., predicting credit risk or market volatility), and customer service (e.g., AI-powered chatbots providing financial advice). For instance, credit card companies use AI algorithms to analyze transaction data in real-time and flag potentially fraudulent activities, protecting customers from financial losses.

Autonomous vehicles represent another significant application of AI. These vehicles rely on a complex array of AI technologies, including computer vision (to perceive the environment), sensor fusion (to integrate data from various sensors like cameras, lidar, and radar), path planning (to determine the optimal route), and decision-making (to navigate safely in complex traffic scenarios). Companies like Waymo (waymo.com) and Tesla (tesla.com/autopilot) are at the forefront of developing and testing autonomous vehicle technology. Levandowski (2017) highlights the challenges and potential of autonomous vehicles, noting that "Self-driving cars have the potential to revolutionize transportation, making it[12] safer, more efficient, and more accessible." (p. 54). A potential question readers might have is about the ethical and societal implications of AI in these fields. In healthcare, concerns about data privacy and the potential for algorithmic bias in diagnosis and treatment are important considerations. In finance, the use of AI in trading raises questions about market stability and fairness. In autonomous vehicles, ethical dilemmas arise in situations where the vehicle has to make split-second decisions that could have life-or-death consequences. Addressing these ethical and societal implications through careful regulation, ongoing research, and public discourse is crucial for the responsible development and deployment of AI technologies.

Chapter 6: AI and Human Interaction

6.1 Human-AI Collaboration: Chatbots, Virtual Assistants, and Robotics

The relationship between humans and artificial intelligence is increasingly characterized by collaboration, where AI systems augment human capabilities and assist in various tasks. This collaboration is evident in the proliferation of chatbots, virtual assistants, and advanced robotics. Chatbots, powered by Natural Language Processing (NLP), interact with humans through text or voice, providing customer support, answering queries, and guiding users through processes. For instance, many e-commerce websites now employ chatbots to handle common customer inquiries, such as tracking orders or providing product information, freeing up human agents to deal with more complex issues. Virtual assistants, like Apple's Siri, Amazon's Alexa, and Google Assistant, integrate NLP and AI to perform tasks based on voice commands, ranging from setting reminders and playing music to controlling smart home devices. These assistants learn user preferences over time, becoming more personalized and efficient.

Robotics has also witnessed a significant shift towards human-robot collaboration, particularly in industrial and service sectors. Collaborative robots, or "cobots," are designed to work alongside humans in shared workspaces, performing tasks that are either too dangerous, too repetitive, or require high precision. In manufacturing, for example, cobots can assist human workers in assembly line tasks, increasing efficiency and reducing the risk of injury. In healthcare, robots are being used to assist with surgeries, provide physical therapy, and even deliver medication in hospitals. Parasuraman and Riley (1997) highlight the importance of human factors in designing such collaborative systems, stating that "automation should be designed to enhance human performance, not replace it entirely" (p. 230). A potential question readers might have is regarding the challenges of designing effective human-AI collaboration. Trust, transparency, and the ability for humans to easily understand the AI's reasoning and actions are crucial for successful collaboration. Ensuring seamless communication and intuitive interfaces is also paramount. For example, developing chatbots that can handle complex or ambiguous queries requires advanced NLP techniques and careful design of dialogue flows. One practical way to explore chatbot interaction is through platforms like Dialogflow (dialogflow.cloud.google.com), which allows users to build their own conversational AI agents.

A basic step-by-step guide to creating a simple chatbot with Dialogflow involves:

1. Signing up for a Google Cloud account and accessing the Dialogflow console.
2. Creating a new agent and defining intents, which represent the user's intentions (e.g., "book a flight").
3. Adding training phrases that users might say to express these intents (e.g., "I want to book a flight to London").

4. Defining entities, which are the parameters that the chatbot needs to fulfill an intent (e.g., destination, date).
5. Creating responses that the chatbot will provide to the user. 6. Testing the chatbot using the built-in simulator.

6.2 AI in Creativity: Art, Music, and Content Generation

While traditionally viewed as a uniquely human domain, creativity is increasingly being explored and even replicated by AI systems. AI algorithms are now capable of generating original artwork, composing music, and even writing articles or scripts. In the realm of visual arts, AI models like DALL-E 2 (openai.com/dall-e-2/) and Midjourney (midjourney.com) can create highly detailed and imaginative images from textual descriptions. These models utilize deep learning techniques, particularly generative adversarial networks (GANs) and transformer networks, to learn the patterns and structures of vast datasets of images and then generate new, unseen images based on user prompts. For example, a user could prompt DALL-E 2 to create "a surreal painting of a cat riding a bicycle through a cityscape made of books," and the AI would generate a unique image based on this description.

Similarly, AI is making waves in music composition. Tools like Amper Music (ampermusic.com, now part of Shutterstock) and Google's Magenta (magenta.tensorflow.org) use machine learning to compose original musical pieces in various styles, from classical to electronic. These systems can learn musical rules and patterns from large datasets of music and then generate new melodies, harmonies, and rhythms. AI is also being used for content generation in writing. Tools like GPT-3 and its successor, developed by OpenAI, can generate human-quality text for various purposes, including writing articles, creating marketing copy, and even drafting code. Boden (2004) explores the philosophical implications of AI creativity, arguing that while AI can produce novel outputs, the question of whether it truly possesses creativity in the human sense is still debated (p. 1). A potential question readers might have is whether AI-generated art or music can be considered truly creative. This is a complex philosophical debate that touches upon the nature of creativity, originality, and the role of intention and emotion in the creative process. While AI can undoubtedly produce novel and aesthetically pleasing outputs, some argue that true creativity requires consciousness and subjective experience, which current AI systems lack. Experimenting with AI art generation can be done using platforms like Nightcafe Creator (nightcafe.studio), which offers various AI art generation tools.

A basic step-by-step guide to creating AI art with Nightcafe Creator involves:

1. Signing up for an account on the Nightcafe Creator website.
2. Clicking "Create" and selecting an AI art generation method (e.g., Stable Diffusion, DALL-E 2).
3. Entering a text prompt describing the image you want to create (e.g., "a futuristic cityscape at sunset").
4. Choosing artistic styles, aspect ratios, and other settings.
5. Clicking "Create" to generate the image.

6.3 AI Ethics: Bias, Fairness, and Responsibility

As AI systems become more integrated into our lives, ethical considerations surrounding their development and deployment are increasingly important. Key ethical concerns include bias, fairness, and responsibility. AI bias occurs when an AI system systematically and unfairly discriminates against[1] certain individuals or groups. This bias can arise from biased training data, where the data used to train the AI model reflects existing societal biases. For example, if a facial recognition system is primarily trained on images of one demographic group, it may perform poorly on individuals from other groups, leading to unfair or inaccurate results.

Fairness in AI aims to ensure that AI systems treat all individuals and groups equitably, without discrimination based on protected characteristics like race, gender, or religion. Defining and achieving fairness in AI is a complex challenge, as different notions of fairness can sometimes conflict with each other. For instance, a system that aims for equal accuracy across all groups might still result in different error rates for different groups. Responsibility in AI refers to the question of who is accountable when an AI system makes a mistake or causes harm. This is particularly challenging in complex AI systems where the decision-making process might not be easily interpretable. If a self-driving car causes an accident, for example, who is responsible – the car manufacturer, the software developer, or the owner of the vehicle? Floridi et al. (2018) emphasize the need for a human-centered approach to AI ethics, advocating for principles like beneficence, non-maleficence, autonomy, and justice (p. 690). A potential question readers might have is how to mitigate bias and ensure fairness in AI systems. One approach is to carefully curate and preprocess training data to ensure it is representative and does not reflect existing biases. Another approach involves using algorithmic fairness techniques to modify the AI model or its outputs to reduce bias. Transparency and interpretability of AI models are also crucial for identifying and addressing potential biases. For instance, using explainable AI (XAI) techniques can help understand why an AI model made a particular decision. Exploring resources like the Partnership on AI (partnershiponai.org) can provide insights into ongoing efforts to address AI ethics. Their work often involves developing guidelines and best practices for responsible AI development and deployment.

6.4 Future of Work: AI's Impact on Jobs and Society

The rapid advancements in AI are expected to have a profound impact on the future of work and society as a whole. While AI has the potential to automate many tasks currently performed by humans, leading to[2] increased efficiency and productivity, it also raises concerns about job displacement[3] and the need for workforce adaptation. Some studies predict that AI and automation could lead to significant job losses in certain sectors, particularly those involving routine or manual tasks. For example, the increasing automation of manufacturing processes through robotics and AI-powered systems is already transforming the nature of work in factories.

However, many experts also argue that AI will not simply replace jobs but will rather augment human capabilities and create new types of jobs that do not currently exist. The focus is likely to shift towards tasks that require uniquely human skills, such as creativity, critical thinking, emotional[4] intelligence, and complex problem-solving. For instance, while AI might automate data analysis, human experts will still be needed to interpret the results and make strategic decisions. Brynjolfsson and McAfee (2014) discuss the "second machine age," arguing that we are entering a period of unprecedented technological change that will transform the economy and society in profound ways (p. 7). A potential question readers might have is how individuals and society can prepare for the future of work in the age of AI. Lifelong learning and upskilling will be crucial for workers to adapt to the changing demands of the job market. Education systems may need to evolve to focus more on developing skills that are less likely to be automated, such as creativity and critical thinking. Governments and organizations may also need to consider policies and initiatives to support workers during this transition, such as providing retraining programs or exploring universal basic income. Furthermore, the societal implications of widespread AI adoption, including issues of economic inequality, social equity, and the ethical use of AI, will need careful consideration and proactive solutions to ensure a positive future for all.

Chapter 7: Cutting-Edge AI Technologies and Innovations

7.1 Generative AI: GPT, Llama, and Diffusion Models

Generative AI represents a fascinating frontier in artificial intelligence, focused on creating models that can generate new, realistic data samples that resemble the data they were trained on. Unlike discriminative models that learn to distinguish between different classes or predict outcomes, generative models learn the underlying probability distribution of the training data, enabling them to produce novel content. Several architectures have gained prominence in this field, including transformer-based models like GPT (Generative Pre-trained Transformer) and Llama (Large Language Model Meta AI), as well as diffusion models.

GPT models, pioneered by OpenAI, have demonstrated remarkable capabilities in natural language generation. Trained on massive datasets of text and code, they can generate coherent and contextually relevant text for a wide range of tasks, from writing articles and poems to answering questions and even generating code. For instance, GPT-4 (openai.com/gpt-4/) can produce remarkably human-like text and has been integrated into various applications, such as writing assistants and chatbots. Llama, developed by Meta AI, is another powerful large language model that has gained significant traction in the research community due to its open access and competitive performance. These models leverage the transformer architecture, which excels at capturing long-range dependencies in sequential data like text.

Diffusion models have emerged as a state-of-the-art approach for image and video generation. Unlike GANs (Generative Adversarial Networks), which were previously dominant in this area, diffusion models work by gradually adding noise to the training data (the forward diffusion process) and then learning to reverse this process to generate new samples from noise (the reverse diffusion process). This approach has led to the creation of highly realistic and diverse images by models like DALL-E 2 and Stable Diffusion (stablediffusion.com). For example, Stable Diffusion allows users to generate high-quality images from text prompts, with a wide range of artistic styles and subjects. A practical way to experience the capabilities of such models is through online platforms. For instance, Hugging Face (huggingface.co) provides access to numerous pre-trained generative AI models and interactive demos.

A step-by-step guide to trying out a text generation model on Hugging Face might involve:

1. Navigating to the Hugging Face website and exploring the "Models" section.
2. Searching for a text generation model, such as "gpt2" or a fine-tuned version.
3. Selecting a model and clicking on the "Use in Spaces" or "Inference API" tab.
4. Typing a prompt or initial text into the provided interface.
5. Clicking "Run" or a similar button to generate the model's output.

Radford et al. (2018) introduced the original GPT model and highlighted the potential of pre-trained language models for various NLP tasks. A potential question readers might have is about the limitations and potential misuse of generative AI. Concerns exist regarding the generation of biased or harmful content, the potential for misuse in creating deepfakes, and the impact on creative industries. Responsible development and deployment of these technologies are crucial, involving ethical guidelines, detection mechanisms, and ongoing research into mitigating these risks.

7.2 AI and IoT: Smart Homes, Smart Cities, and Autonomous Systems

The convergence of Artificial Intelligence (AI) and the Internet of Things (IoT) is driving innovation across various domains, leading to the development of smart homes, smart cities, and autonomous systems. IoT involves a network of physical devices, vehicles, buildings, and other items embedded with sensors, software, and connectivity which enables[1] these objects to collect and exchange data. When AI is integrated with IoT, it enables these connected devices to analyze data locally or in the cloud, make intelligent decisions, and automate actions without direct human intervention.

Smart homes exemplify this synergy, where IoT devices like smart thermostats (e.g., Nest, nest.com), smart lighting systems (e.g., Philips Hue, philips-hue.com), and smart security cameras (e.g., Ring, ring.com) collect data about the home environment and user behavior. AI algorithms can then analyze this data to optimize energy consumption, personalize lighting preferences, and enhance home security. For instance, a smart thermostat can learn a user's preferred temperature settings at different times of the day and automatically[2] adjust the temperature accordingly.

The concept of smart cities takes this integration to a larger scale, applying AI and IoT technologies to improve urban living. This includes intelligent traffic management systems that use AI to optimize traffic flow based on real-time data from sensors, smart grids that can predict energy demand and manage distribution efficiently, and smart waste management systems that optimize collection routes based on fill levels in bins. Batty et al. (2012) discuss the potential of smart cities to address urban challenges through the use of information and communication technologies. Autonomous systems, such as self-driving cars and drones, represent another significant application of AIoT. These systems rely on a combination of sensors (IoT devices) to perceive their surroundings and sophisticated AI algorithms to process this data, make decisions, and navigate autonomously. For example, autonomous vehicles use lidar, radar, and cameras to create a detailed understanding of their environment, and AI algorithms then process this information to control the vehicle's movement. A potential question readers might have is about data privacy and security in AIoT environments. The proliferation of connected devices collecting vast amounts of personal data raises significant concerns about privacy and the potential for security breaches. Ensuring the security of these devices and the data they collect is crucial, requiring robust encryption, secure communication protocols, and careful consideration of data governance policies. Exploring platforms like AWS IoT Core (aws.amazon.com/iot-core/) can provide insights into the infrastructure required to build and manage IoT solutions.

A basic step-by-step guide to connecting a simple sensor to AWS IoT Core might involve:

1. Creating an AWS account and navigating to the AWS IoT Core service.
2. Creating a new "thing" which represents your physical device.
3. Downloading the AWS IoT device SDK for your chosen programming language (e.g., Python).
4. Writing code on your device to connect to AWS IoT Core using the SDK and the credentials associated with your "thing."
5. Publishing data from your sensor to a specific MQTT topic in AWS IoT Core.
6. Optionally, setting up rules in AWS IoT Core to process the incoming data and trigger actions.

7.3 Quantum AI: The Future of Supercomputing

Quantum computing, a paradigm that leverages the principles of quantum mechanics to perform computations, holds the potential to revolutionize various fields, including artificial intelligence. While classical computers store information as bits, which can be either 0 or 1, quantum computers use qubits, which can exist in a superposition[3] of both states simultaneously. This, along with other quantum phenomena like entanglement, allows quantum computers to perform certain calculations much faster than even the most powerful classical supercomputers. The application of quantum computing to AI, often referred to as Quantum AI, is an emerging field with the potential to significantly enhance the capabilities of machine learning algorithms.

One area where Quantum AI could have a major impact is in optimization problems, which are common in AI applications like training complex neural networks, logistics, and financial modeling. Quantum algorithms like the Quantum Approximate Optimization Algorithm (QAOA) show promise in finding optimal or near-optimal solutions to these problems more efficiently than classical algorithms. Another potential application is in quantum machine learning, where quantum algorithms are developed to speed up or improve the performance of machine learning tasks. For example, quantum algorithms for tasks like dimensionality reduction and classification are being actively researched. Harrow, Hassidim, and Lloyd (2009) presented an early quantum algorithm for solving linear systems exponentially faster than the best classical algorithms, highlighting the potential for quantum speedups in machine learning. While quantum computers are still in their early stages of development, with limitations in the number and stability of qubits, significant progress is being made by companies like IBM (ibm.com/quantum-computing/), Google (quantumai.google/), and Microsoft (quantum.microsoft.com/). A potential question readers might have is about the timeline for widespread adoption of Quantum AI. It is generally acknowledged that quantum computing is still several years away from being widely accessible and mature enough to tackle complex real-world AI problems.

However, researchers are actively working on improving qubit stability, increasing qubit counts, and developing new quantum algorithms. Exploring the resources and educational materials provided by these leading companies can offer a glimpse into the current state and future directions of quantum computing. For instance, IBM Quantum Experience (quantum-computing.ibm.com/) provides access to real quantum hardware and a cloud-based platform for running quantum algorithms.

A basic step-by-step guide to running a simple quantum circuit on IBM Quantum Experience involves:

1. Creating an IBM Quantum Experience account.
2. Accessing the Quantum Composer, a visual interface for building quantum circuits.
3. Dragging and dropping quantum gates (like Hadamard, Pauli-X, CNOT) onto qubits.
4. Connecting the qubits and gates to create a quantum circuit.
5. Running the circuit on a simulator or real quantum hardware.
6. Observing the measurement outcomes.

7.4 Artificial General Intelligence (AGI): Will Machines Think Like Humans?

Artificial General Intelligence (AGI), sometimes referred to as strong AI, represents the hypothetical ability of an[4] intelligent agent to understand or learn any intellectual[5] task that a human being can. Unlike narrow AI, which is designed for specific tasks, AGI would possess human-level cognitive abilities across a wide range of domains, including reasoning, learning, planning, creativity, and understanding natural language. The pursuit of AGI is a long-term goal of AI research and is often the subject of philosophical debates and science fiction.

While significant progress has been made in narrow AI, achieving AGI remains a formidable challenge. The complexity of the human brain and the intricacies of human consciousness are not yet fully understood, making it difficult to replicate these in a machine. Current AI models, even the most advanced ones, still lack the general-purpose intelligence and adaptability of humans. They excel in specific tasks but struggle with novel situations or tasks outside their training domain. Bostrom (2014) provides a comprehensive analysis of the potential risks and benefits of AGI, highlighting the profound implications it could have for humanity. A potential question readers might have is about the timeline for when AGI might be achieved. There is no consensus among AI researchers on when or even if AGI will be realized. Estimates range from decades to centuries, and some researchers believe it may not be achievable at all with our current understanding of intelligence and computation. However, the rapid pace of progress in AI, particularly in areas like deep learning, continues to fuel research and speculation about the possibility of AGI in the future. Exploring the work of organizations like the OpenAI Alignment team (openai.com/alignment/) and DeepMind's research (deepmind.com/research/) can provide insights into the current efforts and challenges in the pursuit of more general and human-like artificial intelligence. The development of AGI would raise profound ethical, societal, and philosophical questions that would need careful consideration and global collaboration.

Chapter 7: Cutting-Edge AI Technologies and Innovations

7.1 Generative AI: GPT, Llama, and Diffusion Models

Generative AI represents a fascinating frontier in artificial intelligence, focused on creating models that can generate new, realistic data samples that resemble the data they were trained on. Unlike discriminative models that learn to distinguish between different classes or predict outcomes, generative models learn the underlying probability distribution of the training data, enabling them to produce novel content. Several architectures have gained prominence in this field, including transformer-based models like GPT (Generative Pre-trained Transformer) and Llama (Large Language Model Meta AI), as well as diffusion models.

GPT models, pioneered by OpenAI, have demonstrated remarkable capabilities in natural language generation. Trained on massive datasets of text and code, they can generate coherent and contextually relevant text for a wide range of tasks, from writing articles and poems to answering questions and even generating code. For instance, GPT-4 (openai.com/gpt-4/) can produce remarkably human-like text and has been integrated into various applications, such as writing assistants and chatbots. Llama, developed by Meta AI, is another powerful large language model that has gained significant traction in the research community due to its open access and competitive performance. These models leverage the transformer architecture, which excels at capturing long-range dependencies in sequential data like text.

Diffusion models have emerged as a state-of-the-art approach for image and video generation. Unlike GANs (Generative Adversarial Networks), which were previously dominant in this area, diffusion models work by gradually adding noise to the training data (the forward diffusion process) and then learning to reverse this process to generate new samples from noise (the reverse diffusion process). This approach has led to the creation of highly realistic and diverse images by models like DALL-E 2 and Stable Diffusion (stablediffusion.com). For example, Stable Diffusion allows users to generate high-quality images from text prompts, with a wide range of artistic styles and subjects. A practical way to experience the capabilities of such models is through online platforms. For instance, Hugging Face (huggingface.co) provides access to numerous pre-trained generative AI models and interactive demos.

A step-by-step guide to trying out a text generation model on Hugging Face might involve:

1. Navigating to the Hugging Face website and exploring the "Models" section.
2. Searching for a text generation model, such as "gpt2" or a fine-tuned version.
3. Selecting a model and clicking on the "Use in Spaces" or "Inference API" tab.
4. Typing a prompt or initial text into the provided interface.
5. Clicking "Run" or a similar button to generate the model's output.

Radford et al. (2018) introduced the original GPT model and highlighted the potential of pre-trained language models for various NLP tasks. A potential question readers might have is about the limitations and potential misuse of generative AI. Concerns exist regarding the generation of biased or harmful content, the potential for misuse in creating deepfakes, and the impact on creative industries. Responsible development and deployment of these technologies are crucial, involving ethical guidelines, detection mechanisms, and ongoing research into mitigating these risks.

7.2 AI and IoT: Smart Homes, Smart Cities, and Autonomous Systems

The convergence of Artificial Intelligence (AI) and the Internet of Things (IoT) is driving innovation across various domains, leading to the development of smart homes, smart cities, and autonomous systems.[7] IoT involves a network of physical devices, vehicles, buildings, and other items embedded with sensors, software, and connectivity which enables these objects to collect and exchange data. When AI is integrated with IoT, it enables these connected devices to analyze data locally or in the cloud, make intelligent decisions, and automate actions without direct human intervention.

Smart homes exemplify this synergy, where IoT devices like smart thermostats (e.g., Nest, nest.com), smart lighting systems (e.g., Philips Hue, philips-hue.com), and smart security cameras (e.g., Ring, ring.com) collect data about the home environment and user behavior. AI algorithms can then analyze this data to optimize energy consumption, personalize lighting preferences, and[8] enhance home security. For instance, a smart thermostat can learn a user's preferred temperature settings at different times of the day and automatically adjust the temperature accordingly.

The concept of smart cities takes this integration to a larger scale, applying AI and IoT technologies to improve urban living. This includes intelligent traffic management systems that use AI to optimize traffic flow based on real-time data from sensors, smart grids that can predict energy demand and manage distribution efficiently, and smart waste management systems that optimize collection routes based on fill levels in bins. Batty et al. (2012) discuss the potential of smart cities to address urban challenges through the use of information and communication technologies. Autonomous systems, such as self-driving cars and drones, represent another significant application of AIoT. These systems rely on a combination of sensors (IoT devices) to perceive their surroundings and sophisticated AI algorithms to process this data, make decisions, and navigate autonomously. For example, autonomous vehicles use lidar, radar, and cameras to create a detailed understanding of their environment, and AI algorithms then process this information to control the vehicle's movement. A potential question readers might have is about data privacy and security in AIoT environments. The proliferation of connected devices collecting vast amounts of personal data raises significant concerns about privacy and the potential for security breaches. Ensuring the security of these devices and the data they collect is crucial, requiring robust encryption, secure communication protocols, and careful consideration of data governance policies. Exploring platforms like AWS IoT Core (aws.amazon.com/iot-core/) can provide insights into the infrastructure required to build and manage IoT solutions.

A basic step-by-step guide to connecting a simple sensor to AWS IoT Core might involve:

1. Creating an AWS account and navigating to the AWS IoT Core service.
2. Creating a new "thing" which represents your physical device.
3. Downloading the AWS IoT device SDK for your chosen programming language (e.g., Python).
4. Writing code on your device to connect to AWS IoT Core using the SDK and the credentials associated with your "thing."
5. Publishing data from your sensor to a specific MQTT topic in AWS IoT Core.
6. Optionally, setting up rules in AWS IoT Core to process the incoming data and trigger actions.

7.3 Quantum AI: The Future of Supercomputing

Quantum computing, a paradigm that leverages the principles of quantum mechanics to perform computations, holds the potential to revolutionize various fields, including artificial intelligence.[9] While classical computers store information as bits, which can be either 0 or 1, quantum computers use qubits, which can exist in a superposition of both states simultaneously. This, along with other quantum phenomena like entanglement, allows quantum computers to perform certain calculations much faster than even the most powerful classical supercomputers. The application of quantum computing to AI, often referred to as Quantum AI, is an emerging field with the potential to significantly enhance the capabilities of machine learning algorithms.

One area where Quantum AI could have a major impact is in optimization problems, which are common in AI applications like training complex neural networks, logistics, and financial modeling. Quantum algorithms like the Quantum Approximate Optimization Algorithm (QAOA) show promise in finding optimal or near-optimal solutions to these problems more efficiently than classical algorithms. Another potential application is in quantum machine learning, where quantum algorithms are developed to speed up or improve the performance of machine learning tasks. For example, quantum algorithms for tasks like dimensionality reduction and classification are being actively researched. Harrow, Hassidim, and Lloyd (2009) presented an early quantum algorithm for solving linear systems exponentially faster than the best classical algorithms, highlighting the potential for quantum speedups in machine learning. While quantum computers are still in their early stages of development, with limitations in the number and stability of qubits, significant progress is being made by companies like IBM (ibm.com/quantum-computing/), Google (quantumai.google/), and Microsoft (quantum.microsoft.com/). A potential question readers might have is about the timeline for widespread adoption of Quantum AI. It is generally acknowledged that quantum computing is still several years away from being widely accessible and mature enough to tackle complex real-world AI problems.

However, researchers are actively working on improving qubit stability, increasing qubit counts, and developing new quantum algorithms. Exploring the resources and educational materials provided by these leading companies can offer a glimpse into the current state and future directions of quantum computing. For instance, IBM Quantum Experience (quantum-computing.ibm.com/) provides access to real quantum hardware and a cloud-based platform for running quantum algorithms.

A basic step-by-step guide to running a simple quantum circuit on IBM Quantum Experience involves:

1. Creating an IBM Quantum Experience account.
2. Accessing the Quantum Composer, a visual interface for building quantum circuits.
3. Dragging and dropping quantum gates (like Hadamard, Pauli-X, CNOT) onto qubits.
4. Connecting the qubits and gates to create a quantum circuit.
5. Running the circuit on a simulator or real quantum hardware.
6. Observing the measurement outcomes.

7.4 Artificial General Intelligence (AGI): Will Machines10 Think Like Humans?

Artificial General Intelligence[11] (AGI), sometimes referred to as strong AI, represents the hypothetical ability of an intelligent agent to understand or learn any intellectual task that a human being can. Unlike narrow AI, which is designed for specific tasks, AGI would possess human-level cognitive abilities across a wide range of domains, including reasoning, learning, planning, creativity, and understanding natural language. The pursuit of AGI is a long-term goal of AI research and is often the subject of philosophical debates and science fiction.

While significant progress has been made in narrow AI, achieving AGI remains a formidable challenge. The complexity of the human brain and the intricacies of human consciousness are not yet fully understood, making it difficult to replicate these in a machine. Current AI models, even the most advanced ones, still lack the general-purpose intelligence and adaptability of humans. They excel in specific tasks but struggle with novel situations or tasks outside their training domain. Bostrom (2014) provides a comprehensive analysis of the potential risks and benefits of AGI, highlighting the profound implications it could have for humanity. A potential question readers might have is about the timeline for when AGI might be achieved. There is no consensus among AI researchers on when or even if AGI will be realized. Estimates range from decades to centuries, and some researchers believe it may not be achievable at all with our current understanding of intelligence and computation. However, the rapid pace of progress in AI, particularly in areas like deep learning, continues to fuel research and speculation about the possibility of AGI in the future. Exploring the work of organizations like the OpenAI Alignment team (openai.com/alignment/) and DeepMind's research (deepmind.com/research/) can provide insights into the current efforts and challenges in the pursuit of more general and human-like artificial intelligence. The development of AGI would raise profound ethical, societal, and philosophical questions that would need careful consideration and global collaboration.

Chapter 8: The Future of IT and AI

8.1 The Metaverse and Extended Reality (XR)

The future of IT is increasingly intertwined with the emergence of immersive digital experiences, primarily through the Metaverse and Extended Reality (XR). The Metaverse, often envisioned as a persistent, interconnected network of virtual environments, represents a potential evolution of the internet where users can interact with digital objects and other users through avatars, blurring the lines between the physical and digital worlds. Extended Reality (XR) is an umbrella term encompassing various immersive technologies, including Virtual Reality (VR), Augmented Reality (AR), and Mixed Reality (MR).[1] VR provides fully immersive digital experiences that shut out the physical world, often using headsets and motion tracking. AR overlays digital information onto the real world, typically through smartphones or specialized glasses, enhancing the user's perception of reality. MR combines elements of both VR and AR, allowing digital and real-world objects to coexist and interact in real-time.

Real-world applications of the Metaverse and XR are rapidly expanding. In education, VR can provide students with immersive learning experiences, such as virtual field trips to historical sites or[2] anatomical dissections without the need for physical specimens. Companies are using VR for employee training in high-risk environments, allowing them to practice procedures safely and effectively. AR is transforming retail, enabling customers to virtually try on clothes or visualize furniture in their homes before making a purchase. For instance, IKEA's Place app (www.ikea.com/us/en/this-room/ikea-place-app-pub39072d61) allows users to place 3D models of IKEA furniture in their actual living spaces using their smartphone cameras.

A step-by-step guide to using the IKEA Place app involves:

1. Downloading the IKEA Place app from your device's app store.
2. Opening the app and granting it camera access.
3. Browse the IKEA product catalog within the app.
4. Selecting a product and pointing your device's camera at the space where you want to place the virtual furniture.
5. The 3D model of the furniture will appear overlaid on your real-world view, allowing you to move and rotate it.

MR is being utilized in fields like healthcare, where surgeons can access patient data and holographic visualizations during operations, enhancing precision and efficiency. Dionisio, Burns, and Gilbert (2013) discuss the potential of immersive technologies in education, noting that "virtual reality can provide authentic and engaging learning experiences that are difficult or impossible to replicate in the real world" (p. 24). A potential question readers might have is about the underlying technologies that power the Metaverse and XR. These include advancements in display technologies, motion tracking sensors, high-bandwidth and low-latency networking (like 5G), and powerful graphics processing units (GPUs) to render complex virtual environments. The development of open standards and interoperability between different virtual platforms will also be crucial for the Metaverse to truly become a seamless and interconnected experience.

8.2 AI for Sustainability and Green Technology

Artificial intelligence is playing an increasingly vital role in addressing environmental challenges and fostering sustainability. AI algorithms can analyze vast amounts of data to optimize resource management, improve the efficiency of renewable energy systems, and accelerate the development of green technologies. In the energy sector, AI is being used to predict energy demand more accurately, allowing for better management of power grids and reducing waste. It can also optimize the performance of solar and wind power plants by forecasting weather patterns and adjusting operations accordingly. For example, companies like Google are using AI to optimize the cooling systems in their data centers, leading to significant energy savings (www.blog.google/technology/sustainability/reducing-data-center-energy-consumption-with-ai/).

AI is also being applied to improve resource management in areas like agriculture and water conservation. Precision agriculture techniques, powered by AI and IoT sensors, can analyze data on soil conditions, weather patterns, and crop health to optimize irrigation, fertilization, and pest control, reducing[3] the environmental impact of farming. In water management, AI can be used to detect leaks in water distribution systems and optimize water usage in urban areas. Furthermore, AI is accelerating the development of new sustainable materials and green technologies.

Machine learning models can analyze the properties of different materials to discover novel, environmentally friendly alternatives to traditional materials. They can also be used to design more efficient batteries for electric vehicles and optimize the performance of carbon capture technologies. Rolnick et al. (2022) highlight the broad potential of AI to address climate change across various sectors, including energy, transportation, and agriculture. A potential question readers might have is about the environmental impact of AI itself, given the significant computational resources required to train large AI models. Researchers are actively working on developing more energy-efficient AI algorithms and hardware, as well as exploring ways to offset the carbon footprint of AI development. For instance, techniques like model pruning and quantization can reduce the size and computational cost of AI models. Exploring initiatives like Green AI (green-ai.org/) can provide more information on efforts to make AI development and deployment more sustainable.

8.3 Preparing for the Future: AI Education and Career Paths

As AI continues to permeate various aspects of our lives and industries, preparing the next generation of IT professionals with the necessary skills and knowledge is paramount. AI education is becoming increasingly crucial for students pursuing careers in Information Technology. This includes not only understanding the theoretical foundations of AI, such as machine learning algorithms and neural networks, but also gaining practical experience in developing and deploying AI applications. Educational institutions are increasingly incorporating AI-related courses and specializations into their IT curricula to meet this growing demand. Online learning platforms like Coursera (www.coursera.org) and edX (www.edx.org) also offer a wide range of courses and certifications in AI and related fields, making it accessible for individuals to learn these skills regardless of their location or background.

A step-by-step guide to starting an AI learning path on Coursera might involve:

1. Creating an account on the Coursera website.
2. Browse the catalog of courses and specializations related to Artificial Intelligence, Machine Learning, or Deep Learning.
3. Enrolling in an introductory course to gain a foundational understanding of the concepts.
4. Progressing through more advanced courses and specializations based on your interests and career goals.
5. Consider pursuing hands-on projects and capstone projects to apply your knowledge and build a portfolio.

The career landscape in IT is also evolving rapidly with the rise of AI. Traditional IT roles are being augmented or transformed by AI, and new roles are emerging that require expertise in AI and related areas. Some potential career paths in the field of AI include AI Engineer, Machine Learning Engineer, Data Scientist, NLP Specialist, Computer Vision Engineer, and AI Ethics Officer. These roles require a strong foundation in computer science, mathematics, and statistics, as well as specialized knowledge in AI techniques and tools. Many industries are actively seeking professionals with these skills, indicating a strong demand for AI expertise in the future job market. Autor (2015) discusses the potential impact of automation on labor markets and the importance of adapting skills to remain relevant. A potential question readers might have is about the specific skills and knowledge that will be most valuable for future IT professionals in the age of AI. Beyond the technical skills mentioned above, soft skills like critical thinking, problem-solving, creativity, and communication will also be increasingly important, as these are the skills that are less likely to be automated and are essential for collaborating with AI systems and addressing complex challenges. Continuous learning and staying updated with the latest advancements in AI will be crucial for long-term career success in this dynamic field.

8.4 Final Thoughts: The Ever-Evolving Role of IT and AI

As we reach the conclusion of this exploration into the foundations and future of Information Technology and Artificial Intelligence, it is clear that these fields are not only rapidly evolving but are also deeply intertwined, shaping the trajectory of our digital world. From the fundamental components of computers and the intricacies of networking to the transformative power of AI and its emerging applications, the landscape of IT is dynamic and constantly presents new opportunities and challenges. The Metaverse and Extended Reality promise to redefine how we interact with digital environments, while AI is proving to be a critical tool in tackling global challenges like sustainability and climate change.

Preparing for this future requires a commitment to continuous learning and adaptation. For IT students and educators, staying abreast of the latest advancements in AI and related technologies is essential. The career paths in IT are diversifying, with a growing demand for professionals who possess both a strong understanding of traditional IT principles and specialized expertise in areas like machine learning, data science, and AI ethics. The integration of AI into various sectors necessitates a thoughtful and responsible approach, addressing ethical considerations such as bias, fairness, and accountability. The ever-evolving role of IT and AI underscores the importance of fostering innovation while also considering the broader societal implications. As we move forward, the collaboration between humans and AI will likely become even more profound, leading to new possibilities and transforming the way we live and work. The journey of IT and AI is far from over, and the future promises even more exciting developments and transformative changes.

Bibliography

Autor, D. H. (2015). Why are there still so many jobs? The history and future of workplace automation. *Journal of Economic Perspectives*, 29(3), 3-30.

Batty, M., Axhausen, K. W., Giannotti, F., Pozdnoukhov, A., Schnabel, M., Martens, K., ... & Ratti, C. (2012). Smart cities of the future. *The European Physical Journal B*, 85(1), 1-13.

Bishop, C. M. (2006). *Pattern recognition and machine learning*. Springer.

Boden, M. A. (2004). *The creative mind: Myths and mechanisms* (2nd ed.). Routledge.

Bostrom, N. (2014). *Superintelligence: Paths, dangers, strategies*. Oxford University Press.

Brynjolfsson, E., & McAfee, A. (2014). *The second machine age: Work, progress, and prosperity in a time of brilliant technologies*. W. W. Norton & Company.

Comer, D. E. (2018). *Internetworking with TCP/IP, Vol. 1: Principles, protocols, and architecture* (6th ed.). Pearson Education.

Dionisio, J. D. N., Burns, M. J., & Gilbert, R. (2013). 3D virtual worlds and immersive learning: Transformative approaches to education. *Journal of Educational Technology & Society*, 16(1), 24-31.

Floridi, L., Cowls, B., Beltramini, M., Saunders, D., & Vayena, E. (2018). An ethical framework for a good AI society: Opportunities, risks, principles, and recommendations. *AI and Society*, 33(4), 689-707.

Fuegi, J., & Hafner, G. N. (2003). Flourishing a new generation: Ada Lovelace, the first computer programmer. *IEEE Annals of the History of*

Computing, 25(4), 7-16.

Harrow, A. W., Hassidim, A., & Lloyd, S. (2009). Quantum algorithm for linear systems of equations. *Physical Review Letters*, 103(15), 150502.

HealthIT.gov. (n.d.). What are the advantages of EHRs? Retrieved from https://www.healthit.gov/faq/what-are-advantages-ehrs

Information Technology Association of America. (n.d.). What is IT? Retrieved from https://www.comptia.org/content/it-careers-paths-and-certifications/it-careers

Jurafsky, D., & Martin, J. H. (2023). *Speech and language processing* (3rd ed. draft).

LeCun, Y., Bengio, Y., & Hinton, G. (2015). Deep learning. *Nature*, 521(7553), 436-444.

Levandowski, A. (2017). *Self-driving cars: The future of transportation*. MIT Press.

Loshin, D. (2013). *Business intelligence: The savvy manager's guide* (2nd ed.). Morgan Kaufmann.

O'Neil, C. (2016). *Weapons of math destruction: How big data increases inequality and threatens democracy*. Crown.

Parasuraman, R., & Riley, V. (1997). Humans and automation: Use of mental models in fault diagnosis. *Human Factors: The Journal of the Human Factors and Ergonomics Society*, 39(2), 230-253.

Provost, F., & Fawcett, T. (2013). *Data science for business: What you need to know about data mining and data-analytic thinking*. O'Reilly Media.

Radford, A., Narasimhan, K., Salimans, T., & Sutskever, I. (2018). Improving language understanding by generative pre-training.

Rolnick, D., Donti, P. L., Kaack, L. H., Kochanski, K., Lacoste, A., Sankaranarayanan, K., ... & Bengio, Y. (2022). Tackling climate change with machine learning. *ACM Computing Surveys (CSUR)*, 55(2), 1-96.

Russell, S. J., & Norvig, P. (2020). *Artificial intelligence: A modern approach* (4th ed.). Pearson Education.

Shi, W., Pallickara, S., & Jiang, K. (2013). Edge computing: Vision and challenges. In *2013 IEEE 6th International Conference on Internet of Things (iThings)* (pp. 37-40). IEEE.

Silberschatz, A., Galvin, P. B., & Gagne, G. (2018). *Operating system concepts* (10th ed.). Wiley.

Sommerville, I. (2011). *Software engineering* (9th ed.). Pearson Education.

Stallings, W., & Case, L. (2016). *Business data communications and networking* (13th ed.). Pearson Education.

Stonebraker, M., & Kemper, A. (2011). On the differences between OLTP and OLAP. *Proceedings of the VLDB Endowment*, 4(1), 80-91.

Tanenbaum, A. S., & Austin, T. (2013). *Structured computer organization* (6th ed.). Pearson Education.

Techopedia. (n.d.). Technology Dictionary. Retrieved from https://www.techopedia.com/dictionary

Topol, E. J. (2019). *Deep medicine: How artificial intelligence can make healthcare human again*. Basic Books.

Verizon. (2023). *2023 Data Breach Investigations Report*. Retrieved from https://www.verizon.com/business/resources/reports/dbir/

Whitman, M. E., & Mattord, H. J. (2020). *Principles of information security* (7th ed.). Cengage Learning.

About The Author

Early Life and Education

Mark John Lado was born on September 24, 1992, in Danao City, Philippines. From an early age, he exhibited a keen interest in technology and education, which would later shape his career. He pursued his Bachelor of Science in Information Systems (BSIS) at Colegio de San Antonio de Padua, where he graduated with a strong foundation in technology and systems analysis. His academic journey continued as he earned a Master's degree in Information Technology (MIT) from the Northern Negros State College of Science and Technology in Sagay City, Philippines. Currently, he is pursuing his Doctorate in Information Technology at the State University of Northern Negros, reflecting his commitment to lifelong learning and professional growth.

Professional Career

Mark has built a diverse and impactful career in education and technology. He currently serves as an Instructor in the College of Technology and Engineering at Cebu Technological University, a role he has held since October 2022. Prior to this, he was a Faculty member in Business Education and Information Systems at Colegio de San Antonio de Padua from 2018 to 2022. His earlier roles include working as a Part-

Time Information Technology Instructor at the University of the Visayas - Danao Branch and as an ICT Coordinator at Carmen Christian School Inc. in 2017.

Research and Innovation

Mark is an active researcher with a focus on applying technology to solve real-world problems. Some of his notable projects include:

1. "Development of a Microprocessor-Based Sensor Network for Monitoring Water Parameters in Tilapia Traponds"
2. "A Wireless Digital Public Address with Voice Alarm and Text-to-Speech Feature for Different Campuses", which was published in Globus: An International Journal of Management & IT

His research contributions highlight his dedication to innovation and his ability to bridge theoretical knowledge with practical applications.

Authorship and Publications

Mark is a prolific author, having written and published multiple books on technology topics. His works include:

1. Mastering CRUD with Flask in 5 Days; Build Python Web Applications - From Novice to...
2. Flask, PostgreSQL, and Bootstrap: Building Data-Driven Web Applications with CRUD...
3. From Model to Web App: A Comprehensive Guide to Building Data-Driven Web...
4. The Beginner's Guide Computer Systems; Principles, Practices, and Troubleshooting:...

5. Flask Web Framework Building Interactive Web Applications with SQLite Database: A...
6. Mastering PC Troubleshooting & Operating Systems: The Modern Landscape of PC...
7. Mastering Flask in 5 Days; From Zero to Deployment: Building Your First Web App:...
8. Data Modeling and Process Analysis; Essential for Technology Analysts and AI...
9. The Echo of the Past; Information Networks from Stone to Silicon and Beyond AI: How...
10. Cybersecurity Essentials Protecting Your Digital Life, Data, and Privacy in a...
11. Mastering PC Troubleshooting and Operating Systems: The Future-Ready...
12. From Idea to Manuscript: A Step-by-Step Guide to Writing Your Nonfiction Book
13. Microprocessor Magic: Unlocking the Potential of Building Projects from Scratch
14. Data Modeling and Process Analysis: A Comprehensive Guide – Volume I
15. Python Data Science Essentials: A Comprehensive Guide to Mastering...
16. Mastering PC Troubleshooting and Operating Systems: A Comprehensive Guide
17. Cybersecurity Confidence: 8 Steps to Master Digital Security and Boost Productivity
18. Embedded Systems: From Historical Development to Modern-

Day Applications

These books are widely recognized and serve as valuable resources for students, hobbyists, and professionals in the IT field. His publications are available on platforms like Amazon and ThriftBooks, further extending his reach and impact

Certifications and Professional Development

Mark has pursued several certifications to enhance his expertise, including:

- Computer Hardware Servicing from Cebu Technological University
- Consumer Electronics Servicing from TESDA

These certifications underscore his commitment to continuous professional development and staying updated with emerging technological trends.

Contributions to IT Education

As an active member of the Philippine Society of Information Technology Educators (PSITE), Mark contributes to advancing IT education standards in the Philippines. His teaching, research, and authorship have made him a respected figure in the academic and IT communities. He is known for his adaptability to emerging technologies, such as AI-driven systems and cybersecurity, ensuring that his work remains relevant and impactful.

Personal Interests

Outside of his professional life, Mark enjoys reading books, spending time at the beach, and engaging in physical activities like inline skating and biking. These hobbies not only help him unwind but also contribute to his overall well-being and creativity.

Legacy and Impact

Mark John Lado's dedication to education, research, and professional excellence has made him a valuable asset to the IT community. His contributions have empowered countless students and professionals, preparing them for the challenges of a rapidly evolving technological landscape. His unwavering passion for technology and continuous pursuit of learning ensure that his legacy will endure for years to come.

For more details about his work, you can visit his official website https://markjohnlado.com/

or explore his publications on Amazon Author Page https://www.amazon.com/stores/author/B0BZM8PM6R

I highly recommend reading this book to further enhance your skills and deepen your understanding of the subject.

https://a.co/d/ahv6VWa

https://a.co/d/b1W3F8n

https://a.co/d/izTWNbO

https://a.co/d/6HHyUFk

www.ingramcontent.com/pod-product-compliance
Lightning Source LLC
LaVergne TN
LVHW051537050326
832903LV00033B/4304

* 9 7 9 8 3 1 6 6 8 9 8 0 4 *